GD24032

A 32bit CPU:

32 registers, 32bit wide

Highly orthogonal instruction set

100 instructions, with conditional execution available for most of them. All instructions may or may not affect flags

DSP-like instructions

13 addressing modes: Immediate, Immediate-8, Register Direct, Register Indirect (with and without base offset, both short and long), Register Indirect with Pre and Post increment, Pre and Post decrement, Register Indirect with 2 registers), Far (64bit) Register Indirect and 2-registers Indirect (with Post increment)

32bit address space, optionally 64

8/16/32/64bit operations

4 CPU modes, User/IRQ/Super; Supervisor and User Stack Pointer available.

32 interrupt levels

Trap handling (30 system and 64 user)

Remappable register set (for fast context switching)

Exception context accessible

Time-stamp register available (64bit wide)

Cache and atomic operations management

20/03/25 13:07

Registers

Registers are numbered from R0 to R31: all registers are general-purpose, except for:

- R31 which is used as Program Counter (Instruction Pointer)
- R30 which is/can be used as a storage for PC when a BL (Branch-and-Link) or BLWP instruction are performed, with subsequent RETU (Return and Unlink) or RTWP
- R29 which is used a storage for WP (Workspace Pointer) when a BLWP (Branch-and-Load Workspace Pointer) instruction is performed, with subsequent RTWP (Return Workspace Pointer)
- R28

Hence, writing to these registers is only allowed when CPU is in Supervisor Mode.

This CPU can operate with two different types of registers:

- when bit 13 of Status Register (Remap Registers) is reset, a single set of 32 registers is available as in most CPUs
- when bit 13 of Status Register (Remap Registers) is set, the 32 registers are mapped in RAM, according to special register WP (Workspace Pointer), allowing for fast context switching

Status is a 32bit word that contains state and setting used in most CPU activities.

Supervisor Stack Pointer and Used Stack Pointer are used to manage the Stack, depending on CPU mode.

Status registers and flags

Status register is 32bit wide and contains flags and settings:
- Z (zero flag) is set when content of destination is Zero, reset otherwise
- S (sign flag) is set when content of destination is Negative, and reset if positive (or zero)
- C (carry flag) is set when the result of an operation won't fit the destination size, causing a Carry-on
- HC (HalfCarry flag) is set when an operation causes a Carry-on from the low nibble (either 4, 8, 16 or 32bit) to the high one
- P (parityflag) is set when the Parity content of destination is Even, reset otherwise (only for byte-sized operands)
- OV (overflow flag) is set when the result of an operation on signed operands causes a change of sign
- AS (add/sub flag) is set according to the type of operation executed
- D (dir flag) is set according to the direction used by a Repeated Instruction
- X (Xop flag) is set when XOP instruction is executed
- NT (nested task flag) is (future extension)
- Priv (privileged instruction flag) is set when a privileged instruction is executed
- IOPL (I/O privileged flag) is (future extension)
- Trap (trap flag) is set when either a System or User trap is executed
- RR (remap register setting) when set, allows Register Remapping
- EA (enforce alignment setting) when set, forces 32bit-aligned memory accesses, causing an exception if unaligned attempts are performed
- A64 (64bit addresses setting) enables 64bit-wide memory addressing
- (next 8 bits are reserved for future extensions)
- T (trace flag) is set when tracing is enabled
- CPU mode (2bit setting) sets CPU execution level, from User (lowest) to Supervisor (highest)
- IRQ mask (5bit setting) sets filter for interrupt execution

All instructions can either affect or not affect arithmetic flags, depending on their opcode.

Only the first 8 bits can be explicitly rewritten (via LDST instruction) when CPU is not in Supervisor Mode; all bits can always be read using STST instruction.

Interrupts and Traps

32 levels of interrupts are available; the Interrupt Mask in Status Registers controls which interrupt levels will be executed or ignored.

A total of 94 Traps (system exceptions/errors and user defined Traps) are available: the first 8 are currently defined as:

Bus Error = 0
Address Error = 1
Illegal Opcode = 2
Divide By Zero = 3
Out of Bounds = 4 (CHK instruction)
Overflow = 5
Privilege Violation = 6
Trace = 7
(others: reserved for future use)

Software Traps from 0 to 63 are available to the user, via TRAP or XOP instructions.

All interrupts and traps use vectors located in the first 1Kbyte of memory area (usually ROM): System Exceptions range from 0x00000010 to 0x000000FF, then Traps go from 0x00000100 to 0x000002FF and in the end Interrupts will use addresses 0x00000300 up to 0x000003FF.
Each vector specifies an address for code and an address for the new WP, in case register remapping is used.

CPU State at the time an exception occurred is fully available via STEX instruction.

Assembler syntax

OPCODE
    Instructions with implicit behaviour

OPCODE [.size][.flags] [condition,] <operand>
    Instructions performing operation on a single operand; standard addressing modes apply

OPCODE [.size][.flags] <destination> , <operand1> , <operand2>
    Instructions performing operation on an operand according to extra parameters; standard addressing modes apply (with some limitations)

OPCODE [.size][.flags] <destination> , <source>
    Instructions performing operation between two operands and storing the result into destination; standard addressing modes apply to both and source can also be an immediate value

OPCODE <destination address>
    Instructions that move Program Counter to a new address; destination address can be either relative (8bit or 17bit) offset or absolute

OPCODE <source or destination address> , <register list>
    Instructions that load or store a list of registers in memory

Size can optionally be specified for these instructions {b, w, d, q}, otherwise it will default to 32bit unless automatically chosen depending upon size of literal operand.
! suffix on addresses means 64bit addressing (if enabled in Status)
Flags may or may not be affected by these instructions, depending on the presence of .f modifier.
A condition may be applied to these instructions, so that they will only be executed if the condition is met.

```
MOV.b [R1],500
MOV.b [R0+R7+100],R2
MOV.b [R1+10000],R1
MOV.b [R1+100],200
MOV.b [R1,100],800
MOV.b [R1!],3500
CLR.d R0
PUSH.b 65
POP.b R0
TRAP 4
LDIM 3<<2

LDWP 0x00010800
STST R1
```

```
CALL ls,delay
MOV.q R0,400005612001
MOV.q R3,R4
LEA R0,stringa

JR testjmp2

CMP.b.f R8,0
BEQ trap4_0

STM (R8++),{R0,R1}
LDM {R0-R2,R5,R7},(R8++)
```

Addressing modes

- Implicit: no addressing is needed/used
- Immediate: a number up 64bit large follows the instruction
- Immediate-8:   an 8bit number is embedded into the instruction (in the lower 8 bits)
- Register: one of the 32 available registers is used (restrictions apply)
- Register Indirect: one of the 32 available registers is used to point to memory
- Symbolic Indexed: a signed 32bit value following the instruction is used to point to memory, optionally adding one of the registers from R1 to R31
- Symbolic Indexed Short: a signed 8bit value embedded in the instruction is used to point to memory, together with one of the 32 registers
- Two Registers indirect: one register plus signed value from another one from R0 to R7 is used as a pointer to memory area
- Register Indirect with Preincrement: one of the 32 available registers is used to point to memory, and its value is incremented before use (increment step depends upon operand size) (restrictions/cautions apply)
- Register Indirect with Predecrement: one of the 32 available registers is used to point to memory, and its value is decremented before use (decrement step depends upon operand size) (restrictions/cautions apply)
- Register Indirect with Postincrement: one of the 32 available registers is used to point to memory, and its value is incremented after use (increment step depends upon operand size) (restrictions/cautions apply)
- Register Indirect with Postdecrement: one of the 32 available registers is used to point to memory, and its value is decremented before use (decrement step depends upon operand size) (restrictions/cautions apply)
- Register-64 Indirect: two consecutive registers (out of the 32 available) are used as pointer to 64bit range memory
- Two Registers Register-64 Indirect: two consecutive registers (out of the 32 available) are used as pointer to 64bit range memory, together with the signed value of a third 32bit register
- Register-64 Indirect with Postincrement: two consecutive registers (out of the 32 available) are used as pointer to 64bit range memory, and that 64bit number is then incremented according to the operand size

Instruction set

All instructions can either affect or skip arithmetic flags.
All privileged instructions will cause a Privilege exception if execution is attempted when CPU is not in Supervisor mode.
Many instructions give the opportunity to only be executed if a condition is met.

NOP   No Operation
Opcode   **00**

Format:

0	0	0	0	0	0	0	x	x	x	x	x	x	x	x	x	x	x	x	x	x	x	x	x	x	x	x	x	x	x	x	x

Performs: No operation

Addressing modes: n/a

Cycles:

Flags affected: none

MOV   Move
Opcode   **01**

Format:

0	0	0	0	0	0	1	F	S	S	x	D	D	D	D	d	d	d	d	d	S	S	S	S	s	s	s	s	s	r	r	r
0	0	0	0	0	0	1	F	0	0	x	D	D	D	D	d	d	d	d	d	0	0	0	0	n	n	n	n	n	n	n	n

Performs: Copies Source into Destination
Operands size: Byte, Word, Double-Word, Quadruple-Word
Addressing modes:
> source: Immediate-8, Immediate, Register, Register Indirect with or without Pre-or-Post-Increment-or-Decrement, Indexed, Register Indexed, Two-Registers Indexed, 64bit Register Indirect, 64bit Two-Registers Indexed, 64bit Register Indirect with Post-Increment
> destination: Register, Register Indirect with or without Pre-or-Post-Increment-or-Decrement, Indexed, Register Indexed, Two-Registers Indexed, Register Short Indexed, 64bit Register Indirect, 64bit Two-Registers Indexed, 64bit Register Indirect with Post-Increment

Cycles:

Flags affected: Zero, Sign, Parity (if F bit is set)

MOVS   Move String
Opcode   **02**

Format:

0	0	0	0	0	1	0	x	S	S	x	D	D	D	D	d	d	d	d	d	S	S	S	S	s	s	s	s	s	R	R	R

Performs: Multiple copies from Source to Destination, using 32bit specified register (R0-R7) as a counter down to zero

Operands size: Byte, Word, Double-Word, Quadruple-Word
Addressing modes:

source: Immediate-8, Immediate, Register, Register Indirect with or without Pre-or-Post-Increment-or-Decrement, Indexed, Register Indexed, Two-Registers Indexed, 64bit Register Indirect, 64bit Two-Registers Indexed, 64bit Register Indirect with Post-Increment
destination: Register Indirect with or without Pre-or-Post-Increment-or-Decrement
counter: Register R0-7

Cycles:

Flags affected: Zero is set when counter reaches 0; Direction is set if decrement is used, reset otherwise; AddSub and HalfCarry are reset

XLAT   Table Lookup
Opcode   **04**

Format:

0	0	0	0	0	0	1	F	S	S	x	D	D	D	D	d	d	d	d	d	S	S	S	S	s	s	s	s	s	r	r	r
0	0	0	0	0	0	1	F	0	0	x	D	D	D	D	d	d	d	d	d	0	0	0	0	n	n	n	n	n	n	n	n

Performs: Reads a value from the address calculated using Destination and Source (adjusted for size) and stores it into destination
Operands size: Byte, Word, Double-Word, Quadruple-Word
Addressing modes:
source: Immediate-8, Immediate, Register, Register Indirect with or without Pre-or-Post-Increment-or-Decrement, Indexed, Register Indexed, Two-Registers Indexed, 64bit Register Indirect, 64bit Two-Registers Indexed, 64bit Register Indirect with Post-Increment
destination: Register, Register Indirect with or without Pre-or-Post-Increment-or-Decrement, Indexed, Register Indexed, Two-Registers Indexed, Register Short Indexed, 64bit Register Indirect, 64bit Two-Registers Indexed, 64bit Register Indirect with Post-Increment

Cycles:

Flags affected: Zero, Sign, Parity (if F bit is set)

XLATB   Table Lookup (byte pointer)
Opcode   **04**

Format:

0	0	0	0	0	0	1	F	S	S	x	D	D	D	D	d	d	d	d	d	S	S	S	S	s	s	s	s	s	r	r	r
0	0	0	0	0	0	1	F	0	0	x	D	D	D	D	d	d	d	d	d	0	0	0	0	n	n	n	n	n	n	n	n

Performs: Reads a value from the address calculated using Destination and Source (byte-sized, adjusted for size) and stores it into destination
Operands size: Byte, Word, Double-Word, Quadruple-Word
Addressing modes:
source: Immediate-8, Register, Register Indirect with or without Pre-or-Post-Increment-or-Decrement, Indexed, Register Indexed, Two-Registers Indexed, 64bit Register Indirect, 64bit Two-Registers Indexed, 64bit Register Indirect with Post-Increment

destination: Register, Register Indirect with or without Pre-or-Post-Increment-or-Decrement, Indexed, Register Indexed, Two-Registers Indexed, Register Short Indexed, 64bit Register Indirect, 64bit Two-Registers Indexed, 64bit Register Indirect with Post-Increment

Cycles:

Flags affected: Zero, Sign, Parity (if F bit is set)

CLR   Clear
Opcode   **05**

Format: | 0 | 0 | 0 | 0 | 1 | 0 | 1 | F | S | S | C | D | D | D | D | d | d | d | d | d | c | c | c | c | n | n | n | n | n | n | n | n |

Performs: Sets Destination to all-zeros (conditional execution is available).
Operands size: Byte, Word, Double-Word, Quadruple-Word
Addressing modes:
 Register, Register Indirect with or without Pre-or-Post-Increment-or-Decrement, Indexed, Register Indexed, Two-Registers Indexed, Register Short Indexed, 64bit Register Indirect, 64bit Two-Registers Indexed, 64bit Register Indirect with Post-Increment

Cycles:

Flags affected: Zero is set, Sign is reset, Parity is set (if F bit is set)

SET   Set
Opcode   **06**

Format: | 0 | 0 | 0 | 0 | 1 | 1 | 0 | F | S | S | C | D | D | D | D | d | d | d | d | d | c | c | c | c | n | n | n | n | n | n | n | n |

Performs: Sets Destination to all-ones (conditional execution is available).
Operands size: Byte, Word, Double-Word, Quadruple-Word
Addressing modes:
 Register, Register Indirect with or without Pre-or-Post-Increment-or-Decrement, Indexed, Register Indexed, Two-Registers Indexed, Register Short Indexed, 64bit Register Indirect, 64bit Two-Registers Indexed, 64bit Register Indirect with Post-Increment

Cycles:

Flags affected: Zero is reset, Sign is set, Parity is set (if F bit is set)

SE   Sign-Extend
Opcode   **07**

Format: | 0 | 0 | 0 | 0 | 1 | 1 | 1 | F | S | S | C | D | D | D | D | d | d | d | d | d | c | c | c | c | x | x | x | x | x | r | r | r |

Performs: Sign extends operand (conditional execution is available).
Operands size: Word, Double-Word, Quadruple-Word
Addressing modes:
   Register, Register Indirect with or without Pre-or-Post-Increment-or-Decrement, Indexed, Register Indexed, Two-Registers Indexed, Register Short Indexed, 64bit Register Indirect, 64bit Two-Registers Indexed, 64bit Register Indirect with Post-Increment

Cycles:

Flags affected: Zero, Sign, Parity (if F bit is set)

DAA   Decimal Adjust Arithmetic
Opcode   **08**

Format: | 0 | 0 | 0 | 1 | 0 | 0 | 0 | F | S | S | C | D | D | D | D | d | d | d | d | d | c | c | c | c | x | x | x | x | x | r | r | r |

Performs: Decimal Adjusts Destination operand (conditional execution is available).
Operands size: Byte, Word, Double-Word, Quadruple-Word
Addressing modes:
   Register, Register Indirect with or without Pre-or-Post-Increment-or-Decrement, Indexed, Register Indexed, Two-Registers Indexed, Register Short Indexed, 64bit Register Indirect, 64bit Two-Registers Indexed, 64bit Register Indirect with Post-Increment

Cycles:

Flags affected: Zero, Sign, Parity (if F bit is set)

SWAP   Swap
Opcode   **09**

Format: | 0 | 0 | 0 | 1 | 0 | 0 | 1 | F | S | S | C | D | D | D | D | d | d | d | d | d | c | c | c | c | x | x | x | x | M | r | r | r |

Performs: Lower part of Operand is swapped with Higher part, or all bytes in a 32bit Operand are rotated turning a Little-endian into a Big-endian and viceversa (conditional execution is available).
Operands size: Byte, Word, Double-Word, Quadruple-Word
Addressing modes:
   Register, Register Indirect with or without Pre-or-Post-Increment-or-Decrement, Indexed, Register Indexed, Two-Registers Indexed, Register Short Indexed, 64bit Register Indirect, 64bit Two-Registers Indexed, 64bit Register Indirect with Post-Increment

Cycles:

Flags affected: Zero, Sign, Parity (if F bit is set)

EX   Exchange

Opcode   **0A**

Format: | 0 | 0 | 0 | 1 | 0 | 1 | 0 | F | S | S | x | D | D | D | D | d | d | d | d | d | S | S | S | S | s | s | s | s | s | r | r | r |

Performs: Exchanges Source with Destination.
Operands size: Byte, Word, Double-Word, Quadruple-Word
Addressing modes:
>source: Register, Register Indirect with or without Pre-or-Post-Increment-or-Decrement, Indexed, Register Indexed, Two-Registers Indexed, 64bit Register Indirect, 64bit Two-Registers Indexed, 64bit Register Indirect with Post-Increment
>destination: Register, Register Indirect with or without Pre-or-Post-Increment-or-Decrement, Indexed, Register Indexed, Two-Registers Indexed, Register Short Indexed, 64bit Register Indirect, 64bit Two-Registers Indexed, 64bit Register Indirect with Post-Increment

Cycles:

Flags affected: Zero, Sign, Parity (if F bit is set)

LEA   Load Effective Address

Opcode   **0B**

Format: | 0 | 0 | 0 | 1 | 0 | 1 | 1 | 0 | 1 | 0 | x | D | D | D | D | d | d | d | d | d | S | S | S | S | s | s | s | s | s | r | r | r |

Performs: Loads Effective Address as specified from source
Addressing modes:
>source: Immediate, Register, Register Indirect with or without Pre-or-Post-Increment-or-Decrement, Indexed, Register Indexed, Two-Registers Indexed, 64bit Register Indirect, 64bit Two-Registers Indexed, 64bit Register Indirect with Post-Increment
>destination: Register, Register Indirect with or without Pre-or-Post-Increment-or-Decrement, Indexed, Register Indexed, Two-Registers Indexed, Register Short Indexed, 64bit Register Indirect, 64bit Two-Registers Indexed, 64bit Register Indirect with Post-Increment

Cycles:

Flags affected: None

PEA   Push Effective Address

Opcode   **0B**

Format: | 0 | 0 | 0 | 1 | 0 | 1 | 1 | 1 | 1 | 0 | x | x | x | x | x | x | x | x | x | x | S | S | S | S | s | s | s | s | s | r | r | r |

Performs: Pushes Effective Address as specified from source onto the Stack
Addressing modes:
  source: Immediate, Register, Register Indirect with or without Pre-or-Post-Increment-or-Decrement, Indexed, Register Indexed, Two-Registers Indexed, 64bit Register Indirect, 64bit Two-Registers Indexed, 64bit Register Indirect with Post-Increment

Cycles:

Flags affected: None

RDTS   Read Timestamp
Opcode   **0C**

Format:

0	0	0	1	1	0	0	F	S	S	x	D	D	D	D	d	d	d	d	d	x	x	x	x	x	x	x	0	x	n	n	n

Performs: Reads Timestamp counter, which increments for every instruction that's executed, into destination.
Operands size: Byte, Word, Double-Word, Quadruple-Word
Addressing modes:
  Register, Register Indirect with or without Pre-or-Post-Increment-or-Decrement, Indexed, Register Indexed, Two-Registers Indexed, Register Short Indexed, 64bit Register Indirect, 64bit Two-Registers Indexed, 64bit Register Indirect with Post-Increment

Cycles:

Flags affected: Zero, Sign, Parity (if F bit is set)

CPUID   Read CPU Id
Opcode   **0C**

Format:

0	0	0	1	1	0	0	F	S	S	x	D	D	D	D	d	d	d	d	d	x	x	x	x	x	x	x	x	1	n	n	n

Performs: Stores CPU id into destination.
Operands size: Byte, Word, Double-Word, Quadruple-Word
Addressing modes:
  Register, Register Indirect with or without Pre-or-Post-Increment-or-Decrement, Indexed, Register Indexed, Two-Registers Indexed, Register Short Indexed, 64bit Register Indirect, 64bit Two-Registers Indexed, 64bit Register Indirect with Post-Increment

Cycles:

Flags affected: Zero, Sign, Parity (if F bit is set)

ADD   Add

Opcode   **10**

Format:

0	0	1	0	0	0	0	F	S	S	x	D	D	D	D	d	d	d	d	d	S	S	S	S	s	s	s	s	s	r	r	r
0	0	1	0	0	0	0	F	0	0	x	D	D	D	D	d	d	d	d	d	0	0	0	0	n	n	n	n	n	n	n	n

Performs: Source is added to Destination.
Operands size: Byte, Word, Double-Word, Quadruple-Word
Addressing modes:
    source: Immediate-8, Immediate, Register, Register Indirect with or without Pre-or-Post-Increment-or-Decrement, Indexed, Register Indexed, Two-Registers Indexed, 64bit Register Indirect, 64bit Two-Registers Indexed, 64bit Register Indirect with Post-Increment
    destination: Register, Register Indirect with or without Pre-or-Post-Increment-or-Decrement, Indexed, Register Indexed, Two-Registers Indexed, Register Short Indexed, 64bit Register Indirect, 64bit Two-Registers Indexed, 64bit Register Indirect with Post-Increment

Cycles:

Flags affected: Zero, Sign, Carry, HalfCarry, Overflow, Parity (if F bit is set)

ADC   Add with Carry

Opcode   **11**

Format:

0	0	1	0	0	0	1	F	S	S	x	D	D	D	D	d	d	d	d	d	S	S	S	S	s	s	s	s	s	r	r	r
0	0	1	0	0	0	1	F	0	0	x	D	D	D	D	d	d	d	d	d	0	0	0	0	n	n	n	n	n	n	n	n

Performs: Source is added to Destination, also with Carry.
Operands size: Byte, Word, Double-Word, Quadruple-Word
Addressing modes:
    source: Immediate-8, Immediate, Register, Register Indirect with or without Pre-or-Post-Increment-or-Decrement, Indexed, Register Indexed, Two-Registers Indexed, 64bit Register Indirect, 64bit Two-Registers Indexed, 64bit Register Indirect with Post-Increment
    destination: Register, Register Indirect with or without Pre-or-Post-Increment-or-Decrement, Indexed, Register Indexed, Two-Registers Indexed, Register Short Indexed, 64bit Register Indirect, 64bit Two-Registers Indexed, 64bit Register Indirect with Post-Increment

Cycles:

Flags affected: Zero, Sign, Carry, HalfCarry, Overflow, Parity (if F bit is set)

SUB   Subtract

Opcode   **12**

Format:

0	0	1	0	0	1	0	F	S	S	x	D	D	D	D	d	d	d	d	d	S	S	S	S	s	s	s	s	s	r	r	r
0	0	1	0	0	1	0	F	0	0	x	D	D	D	D	d	d	d	d	d	0	0	0	0	n	n	n	n	n	n	n	n

Performs: Destination is subtracted from Source.
Operands size: Byte, Word, Double-Word, Quadruple-Word
Addressing modes:
    source: Immediate-8, Immediate, Register, Register Indirect with or without Pre-or-Post-Increment-or-Decrement, Indexed, Register Indexed, Two-Registers Indexed, 64bit Register Indirect, 64bit Two-Registers Indexed, 64bit Register Indirect with Post-Increment
    destination: Register, Register Indirect with or without Pre-or-Post-Increment-or-Decrement, Indexed, Register Indexed, Two-Registers Indexed, Register Short Indexed, 64bit Register Indirect, 64bit Two-Registers Indexed, 64bit Register Indirect with Post-Increment

Cycles:

Flags affected: Zero, Sign, Carry, HalfCarry, Overflow, Parity (if F bit is set)

SBC — Subtract with Carry (borrow)
Opcode 13

Format:

0	0	1	0	0	0	1	0	F	S	S	x	D	D	D	D	d	d	d	d	d	S	S	S	S	s	s	s	s	s	r	r	r
0	0	1	0	0	0	1	1	F	0	0	x	D	D	D	D	d	d	d	d	d	0	0	0	0	n	n	n	n	n	n	n	n

Performs: Destination and Carry flag are subtracted from Source.
Operands size: Byte, Word, Double-Word, Quadruple-Word
Addressing modes:
    source: Immediate-8, Immediate, Register, Register Indirect with or without Pre-or-Post-Increment-or-Decrement, Indexed, Register Indexed, Two-Registers Indexed, 64bit Register Indirect, 64bit Two-Registers Indexed, 64bit Register Indirect with Post-Increment
    destination: Register, Register Indirect with or without Pre-or-Post-Increment-or-Decrement, Indexed, Register Indexed, Two-Registers Indexed, Register Short Indexed, 64bit Register Indirect, 64bit Two-Registers Indexed, 64bit Register Indirect with Post-Increment

Cycles:

Flags affected: Zero, Sign, Carry, HalfCarry, Overflow, Parity (if F bit is set)

CMP — Compare
Opcode 14

Format:

0	0	1	0	1	0	0	F	S	S	x	D	D	D	D	d	d	d	d	d	S	S	S	S	s	s	s	s	s	r	r	r
0	0	1	0	1	0	0	F	0	0	x	D	D	D	D	d	d	d	d	d	0	0	0	0	n	n	n	n	n	n	n	n

Performs: Compares Destination with Source.
Operands size: Byte, Word, Double-Word, Quadruple-Word
Addressing modes:

source: Immediate-8, Immediate, Register, Register Indirect with or without Pre-or-Post-Increment-or-Decrement, Indexed, Register Indexed, Two-Registers Indexed, 64bit Register Indirect, 64bit Two-Registers Indexed, 64bit Register Indirect with Post-Increment
destination: Register, Register Indirect with or without Pre-or-Post-Increment-or-Decrement, Indexed, Register Indexed, Two-Registers Indexed, Register Short Indexed, 64bit Register Indirect, 64bit Two-Registers Indexed, 64bit Register Indirect with Post-Increment

Cycles:

Flags affected: Zero, Sign, Carry, Overflow (if F bit is set)

Note: in this case, source and destination are to be meant as swapped, by comparison with other instructions.

CMPS — Compare String
Opcode **15**

Format:

| 0 | 0 | 1 | 0 | 1 | 0 | 1 | F | S | S | x | D | D | D | D | d | d | d | d | d | S | S | S | S | s | s | s | s | s | r | r | r |

Performs: Sets Destination to all-ones (conditional execution is available).
Operands size: Byte, Word, Double-Word, Quadruple-Word
Addressing modes:
    source: Immediate-8, Immediate, Register, Register Indirect with or without Pre-or-Post-Increment-or-Decrement, Indexed, Register Indexed, Two-Registers Indexed, 64bit Register Indirect, 64bit Two-Registers Indexed, 64bit Register Indirect with Post-Increment
    destination: Register Indirect with or without Pre-or-Post-Increment-or-Decrement
    counter: Register R0-7

Cycles:

Flags affected: Zero is set when counter reaches 0; Direction is set if decrement is used, reset otherwise; AddSub and HalfCarry are reset

Note: in this case, source and destination are to be meant as swapped, by comparison with other instructions.

INC — Increment
Opcode **18**

Format:

| 0 | 0 | 1 | 1 | 0 | 0 | 0 | F | S | S | C | D | D | D | D | d | d | d | d | d | c | c | c | c | x | x | x | x | x | r | r | r |

Performs: Increments Destination (conditional execution is available).

Operands size: Byte, Word, Double-Word, Quadruple-Word
Addressing modes:
    Register, Register Indirect with or without Pre-or-Post-Increment-or-Decrement, Indexed, Register Indexed, Two-Registers Indexed, Register Short Indexed, 64bit Register Indirect, 64bit Two-Registers Indexed, 64bit Register Indirect with Post-Increment

Cycles:

Flags affected: Zero, Sign, Parity, HalfCarry (if F bit is set)

DEC   Decrement
Opcode   **19**

Format:

0	0	1	1	0	0	1	F	S	S	C	D	D	D	D	d	d	d	d	d	c	c	c	c	x	x	x	x	x	r	r	r

Performs: Decrements Destination (conditional execution is available).
Operands size: Byte, Word, Double-Word, Quadruple-Word
Addressing modes:
    Register, Register Indirect with or without Pre-or-Post-Increment-or-Decrement, Indexed, Register Indexed, Two-Registers Indexed, Register Short Indexed, 64bit Register Indirect, 64bit Two-Registers Indexed, 64bit Register Indirect with Post-Increment

Cycles:

Flags affected: Zero, Sign, Parity, HalfCarry (if F bit is set)

MUL   Multiply
Opcode   **1C**

Format:

0	0	1	1	1	0	0	F	S	S	x	D	D	D	D	d	d	d	d	d	S	S	S	S	s	s	s	s	s	r	r	r
0	0	1	1	1	0	0	F	0	0	x	D	D	D	D	d	d	d	d	d	0	0	0	0	n	n	n	n	n	n	n	n

Performs: Multiplies unsigned Source with Destination.
Operands size: Byte, Word, Double-Word, Quadruple-Word
Addressing modes:
    source: Immediate-8, Immediate, Register, Register Indirect with or without Pre-or-Post-Increment-or-Decrement, Indexed, Register Indexed, Two-Registers Indexed, 64bit Register Indirect, 64bit Two-Registers Indexed, 64bit Register Indirect with Post-Increment
    destination: Register, Register Indirect with or without Pre-or-Post-Increment-or-Decrement, Indexed, Register Indexed, Two-Registers Indexed, Register Short Indexed, 64bit Register Indirect, 64bit Two-Registers Indexed, 64bit Register Indirect with Post-Increment

Cycles:

Flags affected: Zero, Sign, Parity, HalfCarry (if F bit is set)

IMUL — Integer (signed) Multiply

Opcode   **1D**

Format:

0	0	1	1	1	0	1	F	S	S	x	D	D	D	D	d	d	d	d	d	S	S	S	S	s	s	s	s	s	r	r	r
0	0	1	1	1	0	1	F	0	0	x	D	D	D	D	d	d	d	d	d	0	0	0	0	n	n	n	n	n	n	n	n

Performs: Multiplies signed Source with Destination.
Operands size: Byte, Word, Double-Word, Quadruple-Word
Addressing modes:

source: Immediate-8, Immediate, Register, Register Indirect with or without Pre-or-Post-Increment-or-Decrement, Indexed, Register Indexed, Two-Registers Indexed, 64bit Register Indirect, 64bit Two-Registers Indexed, 64bit Register Indirect with Post-Increment
destination: Register, Register Indirect with or without Pre-or-Post-Increment-or-Decrement, Indexed, Register Indexed, Two-Registers Indexed, Register Short Indexed, 64bit Register Indirect, 64bit Two-Registers Indexed, 64bit Register Indirect with Post-Increment

Cycles:

Flags affected: Zero, Sign, Parity, HalfCarry (if F bit is set)

DIV — Divide

Opcode   **1E**

Format:

0	0	1	1	1	1	0	F	S	S	x	D	D	D	D	d	d	d	d	d	S	S	S	S	s	s	s	s	s	r	r	r
0	0	1	1	1	1	0	F	0	0	x	D	D	D	D	d	d	d	d	d	0	0	0	0	n	n	n	n	n	n	n	n

Performs: Divides unsigned Destination by Source.
Operands size: Byte, Word, Double-Word, Quadruple-Word

source: Immediate-8, Immediate, Register, Register Indirect with or without Pre-or-Post-Increment-or-Decrement, Indexed, Register Indexed, Two-Registers Indexed, 64bit Register Indirect, 64bit Two-Registers Indexed, 64bit Register Indirect with Post-Increment
destination: Register, Register Indirect with or without Pre-or-Post-Increment-or-Decrement, Indexed, Register Indexed, Two-Registers Indexed, Register Short Indexed, 64bit Register Indirect, 64bit Two-Registers Indexed, 64bit Register Indirect with Post-Increment

Flags affected: Zero, Sign, Parity, HalfCarry (if F bit is set)

Notes: note how operands are swapped respect to most cases

IDIV — Integer (signed) Divide

Opcode 1F

Format:

0	0	1	1	1	1	1	F	S	S	x	D	D	D	D	d	d	d	d	d	S	S	S	S	s	s	s	s	s	r	r	r
0	0	1	1	1	1	1	F	0	0	x	D	D	D	D	d	d	d	d	d	0	0	0	0	n	n	n	n	n	n	n	n

Performs: Divides signed Destination by Source.
Operands size: Byte, Word, Double-Word, Quadruple-Word

source: Immediate-8, Immediate, Register, Register Indirect with or without Pre-or-Post-Increment-or-Decrement, Indexed, Register Indexed, Two-Registers Indexed, 64bit Register Indirect, 64bit Two-Registers Indexed, 64bit Register Indirect with Post-Increment
destination: Register, Register Indirect with or without Pre-or-Post-Increment-or-Decrement, Indexed, Register Indexed, Two-Registers Indexed, Register Short Indexed, 64bit Register Indirect, 64bit Two-Registers Indexed, 64bit Register Indirect with Post-Increment

Flags affected: Zero, Sign, Parity, HalfCarry (if F bit is set)

Notes: note how operands are swapped respect to most cases

OUT — Output to Port

Opcode 20

Format:

0	1	0	0	0	0	0	F	S	S	x	D	D	D	D	d	d	d	d	d	S	S	S	S	s	s	s	s	s	r	r	r
0	1	0	0	0	0	0	F	0	0	x	D	D	D	D	d	d	d	d	d	0	0	0	0	n	n	n	n	n	n	n	n

Performs: Source value is sent to the Data bus, using Destination as address and activating I/O signal.
Operands size: Byte, Double-Word

source: Immediate-8, Immediate, Register, Register Indirect with or without Pre-or-Post-Increment-or-Decrement, Indexed, Register Indexed, Two-Registers Indexed, 64bit Register Indirect, 64bit Two-Registers Indexed, 64bit Register Indirect with Post-Increment
destination: Immediate, Register, Register Indirect with or without Pre-or-Post-Increment-or-Decrement, Indexed, Register Indexed, Two-Registers Indexed, Register Short Indexed, 64bit Register Indirect, 64bit Two-Registers Indexed, 64bit Register Indirect with Post-Increment

Flags affected: Zero, Sign, Parity (if F bit is set)

OUTS — Output String to Port

Opcode 21

Format:

0	1	0	0	0	0	0	F	S	S	x	D	D	D	D	d	d	d	d	d	S	S	S	S	s	s	s	s	s	r	r	r
0	1	0	0	0	0	0	F	0	0	x	D	D	D	D	d	d	d	d	d	0	0	0	0	n	n	n	n	n	n	n	n

Performs: Source value is sent to the Data bus, using Destination as address and activating I/O signal, repeating until counter Register is down to 0.
Operands size: Byte, Double-Word

> source: Register Indirect with or without Pre-or-Post-Increment-or-Decrement
> destination: Immediate, Register, Register Indirect with or without Pre-or-Post-Increment-or-Decrement, Indexed, Register Indexed, Two-Registers Indexed, Register Short Indexed, 64bit Register Indirect, 64bit Two-Registers Indexed, 64bit Register Indirect with Post-Increment
> counter: Register R0-7

Flags affected: Zero is set when counter reaches 0; Direction is set if decrement is used, reset otherwise; AddSub is set

IN   Input from Port
Opcode   **20**

Format:

0	1	0	0	0	0	0	F	S	S	x	D	D	D	D	d	d	d	d	d	S	S	S	S	s	s	s	s	s	r	r	r
0	1	0	0	0	0	0	F	0	0	x	D	D	D	D	d	d	d	d	d	0	0	0	0	n	n	n	n	n	n	n

Performs: Data bus is read into Destination, using Source as address and activating I/O signal.
Operands size: Byte, Double-Word

> source: Immediate-8, Immediate, Register, Register Indirect with or without Pre-or-Post-Increment-or-Decrement, Indexed, Register Indexed, Two-Registers Indexed, 64bit Register Indirect, 64bit Two-Registers Indexed, 64bit Register Indirect with Post-Increment
> destination: Register, Register Indirect with or without Pre-or-Post-Increment-or-Decrement, Indexed, Register Indexed, Two-Registers Indexed, Register Short Indexed, 64bit Register Indirect, 64bit Two-Registers Indexed, 64bit Register Indirect with Post-Increment

Flags affected: Zero, Sign, Parity (if F bit is set)

INS   Input String from Port
Opcode   **21**

Format:

0	1	0	0	0	0	1	F	S	S	x	D	D	D	D	d	d	d	d	d	S	S	S	S	s	s	s	s	s	r	r	r
0	1	0	0	0	0	1	F	0	0	x	D	D	D	D	d	d	d	d	d	0	0	0	0	n	n	n	n	n	n	n

Performs: Data bus is read into Destination, using Source as address and activating I/O signal, repeating until counter Register is down to 0.
Operands size: Byte, Double-Word

> source: Immediate-8, Immediate, Register, Register Indirect with or without Pre-or-Post-Increment-or-Decrement, Indexed, Register Indexed, Two-Registers Indexed, 64bit Register Indirect, 64bit Two-Registers Indexed, 64bit Register Indirect with Post-Increment
> destination: Register Indirect with or without Pre-or-Post-Increment-or-Decrement

counter: Register R0-7

Flags affected: Zero is set when counter reaches 0; Direction is set if decrement is used, reset otherwise; AddSub is set

AND   Logical AND
Opcode   **28**

Format:

```
0 1 0 1 0 0 0 F S S 0 D D D D d d d d d S S S S s s s s s r r r
0 1 0 1 0 0 0 F 0 0 0 D D D D d d d d d 0 0 0 0 n n n n n n n n
```

Performs: Logical AND between Source and Destination.
Operands size: Byte, Word, Double-Word, Quadruple-Word
Addressing modes:
  source: Immediate-8, Immediate, Register, Register Indirect with or without Pre-or-Post-Increment-or-Decrement, Indexed, Register Indexed, Two-Registers Indexed, 64bit Register Indirect, 64bit Two-Registers Indexed, 64bit Register Indirect with Post-Increment
  destination: Register, Register Indirect with or without Pre-or-Post-Increment-or-Decrement, Indexed, Register Indexed, Two-Registers Indexed, Register Short Indexed, 64bit Register Indirect, 64bit Two-Registers Indexed, 64bit Register Indirect with Post-Increment

Cycles:

Flags affected: Zero, Sign, Parity (if F bit is set)

TEST   Logical AND (only flags affected)
Opcode   **28**

Format:

```
0 1 0 1 0 0 0 F S S 1 D D D D d d d d d S S S S s s s s s r r r
0 1 0 1 0 0 0 F 0 0 1 D D D D d d d d d 0 0 0 0 n n n n n n n n
```

Performs: Logical AND between Source and Destination, discarding the result and (optionally) updating flags.
Operands size: Byte, Word, Double-Word, Quadruple-Word
Addressing modes:
  source: Immediate-8, Immediate, Register, Register Indirect with or without Pre-or-Post-Increment-or-Decrement, Indexed, Register Indexed, Two-Registers Indexed, 64bit Register Indirect, 64bit Two-Registers Indexed, 64bit Register Indirect with Post-Increment
  destination: Register, Register Indirect with or without Pre-or-Post-Increment-or-Decrement, Indexed, Register Indexed, Two-Registers Indexed, Register Short Indexed, 64bit Register Indirect, 64bit Two-Registers Indexed, 64bit Register Indirect with Post-Increment

Cycles:

Flags affected: Zero, Sign, Parity (if F bit is set)

OR — Logical OR

Opcode **29**

Format:

0	1	0	1	0	0	1	F	S	S	x	D	D	D	D	d	d	d	d	d	S	S	S	S	s	s	s	s	s	r	r	r
0	1	0	1	0	0	1	F	0	0	x	D	D	D	D	d	d	d	d	d	0	0	0	0	n	n	n	n	n	n	n	n

Performs: Logical OR between Source and Destination.
Operands size: Byte, Word, Double-Word, Quadruple-Word
Addressing modes:
  source: Immediate-8, Immediate, Register, Register Indirect with or without Pre-or-Post-Increment-or-Decrement, Indexed, Register Indexed, Two-Registers Indexed, 64bit Register Indirect, 64bit Two-Registers Indexed, 64bit Register Indirect with Post-Increment
  destination: Register, Register Indirect with or without Pre-or-Post-Increment-or-Decrement, Indexed, Register Indexed, Two-Registers Indexed, Register Short Indexed, 64bit Register Indirect, 64bit Two-Registers Indexed, 64bit Register Indirect with Post-Increment

Cycles:

Flags affected: Zero, Sign, Parity (if F bit is set)

XOR — Logical Exclusive OR

Opcode **2A**

Format:

0	1	0	1	0	1	0	F	S	S	x	D	D	D	D	d	d	d	d	d	S	S	S	S	s	s	s	s	s	r	r	r
0	1	0	1	0	1	0	F	0	0	x	D	D	D	D	d	d	d	d	d	0	0	0	0	n	n	n	n	n	n	n	n

Performs: Logical eXclusive OR between Source and Destination.
Operands size: Byte, Word, Double-Word, Quadruple-Word
Addressing modes:
  source: Immediate-8, Immediate, Register, Register Indirect with or without Pre-or-Post-Increment-or-Decrement, Indexed, Register Indexed, Two-Registers Indexed, 64bit Register Indirect, 64bit Two-Registers Indexed, 64bit Register Indirect with Post-Increment
  destination: Register, Register Indirect with or without Pre-or-Post-Increment-or-Decrement, Indexed, Register Indexed, Two-Registers Indexed, Register Short Indexed, 64bit Register Indirect, 64bit Two-Registers Indexed, 64bit Register Indirect with Post-Increment

Cycles:

Flags affected: Zero, Sign, Parity (if F bit is set)

NAND — Logical Not-AND

Opcode **2B**

Format:

0	1	0	1	0	1	1	F	S	S	x	D	D	D	D	d	d	d	d	d	S	S	S	S	s	s	s	s	s	r	r	r
0	1	0	1	0	1	1	F	0	0	x	D	D	D	D	d	d	d	d	d	0	0	0	0	n	n	n	n	n	n	n	n

Performs: Logical NAND between Source and Destination.
Operands size: Byte, Word, Double-Word, Quadruple-Word
Addressing modes:
> source: Immediate-8, Immediate, Register, Register Indirect with or without Pre-or-Post-Increment-or-Decrement, Indexed, Register Indexed, Two-Registers Indexed, 64bit Register Indirect, 64bit Two-Registers Indexed, 64bit Register Indirect with Post-Increment
> destination: Register, Register Indirect with or without Pre-or-Post-Increment-or-Decrement, Indexed, Register Indexed, Two-Registers Indexed, Register Short Indexed, 64bit Register Indirect, 64bit Two-Registers Indexed, 64bit Register Indirect with Post-Increment

Cycles:

Flags affected: Zero, Sign, Parity (if F bit is set)

NOR   Logical Not-OR
Opcode   **2C**

Format:

0	1	0	1	1	0	0	F	S	S	x	D	D	D	D	d	d	d	d	d	S	S	S	S	s	s	s	s	s	r	r	r
0	1	0	1	1	0	0	F	0	0	x	D	D	D	D	d	d	d	d	d	0	0	0	0	n	n	n	n	n	n	n	n

Performs: Logical NOR between Source and Destination.
Operands size: Byte, Word, Double-Word, Quadruple-Word
Addressing modes:
> source: Immediate-8, Immediate, Register, Register Indirect with or without Pre-or-Post-Increment-or-Decrement, Indexed, Register Indexed, Two-Registers Indexed, 64bit Register Indirect, 64bit Two-Registers Indexed, 64bit Register Indirect with Post-Increment
> destination: Register, Register Indirect with or without Pre-or-Post-Increment-or-Decrement, Indexed, Register Indexed, Two-Registers Indexed, Register Short Indexed, 64bit Register Indirect, 64bit Two-Registers Indexed, 64bit Register Indirect with Post-Increment

Cycles:

Flags affected: Zero, Sign, Parity (if F bit is set)

NEG   Negate
Opcode   **2D**

Format:

0	1	0	1	1	0	1	F	S	S	C	D	D	D	D	d	d	d	d	d	c	c	c	c	x	x	x	x	x	r	r	r

Performs: Negates Destination, 2s complement (conditional execution is available).

Operands size: Byte, Word, Double-Word, Quadruple-Word
Addressing modes:
Register, Register Indirect with or without Pre-or-Post-Increment-or-Decrement, Indexed, Register Indexed, Two-Registers Indexed, Register Short Indexed, 64bit Register Indirect, 64bit Two-Registers Indexed, 64bit Register Indirect with Post-Increment

Cycles:

Flags affected: Zero, Sign, Parity (if F bit is set)

NOT   Bitwise Invert

Opcode   **2E**

Format:

0	1	0	1	1	1	1	0	F	S	S	C	D	D	D	D	d	d	d	d	d	c	c	c	c	x	x	x	x	x	r	r	r

Performs: Negates Destination, 1s complement (conditional execution is available).
Operands size: Byte, Word, Double-Word, Quadruple-Word
Addressing modes:
Register, Register Indirect with or without Pre-or-Post-Increment-or-Decrement, Indexed, Register Indexed, Two-Registers Indexed, Register Short Indexed, 64bit Register Indirect, 64bit Two-Registers Indexed, 64bit Register Indirect with Post-Increment

Cycles:

Flags affected: Zero, Sign, Parity (if F bit is set)

ABS   Absolute Value

Opcode   **2F**

Format:

0	1	0	1	1	1	1	1	F	S	S	C	D	D	D	D	d	d	d	d	d	c	c	c	c	x	x	x	x	x	r	r	r

Performs: Calculates Absolute value of Destination (conditional execution is available).
Operands size: Byte, Word, Double-Word, Quadruple-Word
Addressing modes:
Register, Register Indirect with or without Pre-or-Post-Increment-or-Decrement, Indexed, Register Indexed, Two-Registers Indexed, Register Short Indexed, 64bit Register Indirect, 64bit Two-Registers Indexed, 64bit Register Indirect with Post-Increment

Cycles:

Flags affected: Zero, Sign, Parity (if F bit is set)

SBZ   **Set Bit to Zero**

Opcode   **30**

Format:

0	1	1	0	0	0	0	F	S	S	T	D	D	D	D	d	d	d	d	d	S	S	S	S	s	s	s	s	r	r	r
0	1	1	0	0	0	0	F	S	S	T	D	D	D	D	d	d	d	d	d	0	0	0	0	n	n	n	n	n	n	n

Performs: Resets Bit to Zero into Destination, as specified by Source (optionally testing it before).
Operands size: Byte, Word, Double-Word, Quadruple-Word
Addressing modes:
> source: Immediate-8, Immediate, Register, Register Indirect with or without Pre-or-Post-Increment-or-Decrement, Indexed, Register Indexed, Two-Registers Indexed, 64bit Register Indirect, 64bit Two-Registers Indexed, 64bit Register Indirect with Post-Increment
> destination: Register, Register Indirect with or without Pre-or-Post-Increment-or-Decrement, Indexed, Register Indexed, Two-Registers Indexed, Register Short Indexed, 64bit Register Indirect, 64bit Two-Registers Indexed, 64bit Register Indirect with Post-Increment

Cycles:

Flags affected: Zero is set if Destination=0 and reset otherwise; HalfCarry is set and AddSub is reset (if F bit is set)

SBO   **Set Bit to One**

Opcode   **31**

Format:

0	1	1	0	0	0	1	F	S	S	T	D	D	D	D	d	d	d	d	d	S	S	S	S	s	s	s	s	r	r	r
0	1	1	0	0	0	1	F	S	S	T	D	D	D	D	d	d	d	d	d	0	0	0	0	n	n	n	n	n	n	n

Performs: Sets Bit to One into Destination, as specified by Source (optionally testing it before).
Operands size: Byte, Word, Double-Word, Quadruple-Word
Addressing modes:
> source: Immediate-8, Immediate, Register, Register Indirect with or without Pre-or-Post-Increment-or-Decrement, Indexed, Register Indexed, Two-Registers Indexed, 64bit Register Indirect, 64bit Two-Registers Indexed, 64bit Register Indirect with Post-Increment
> destination: Register, Register Indirect with or without Pre-or-Post-Increment-or-Decrement, Indexed, Register Indexed, Two-Registers Indexed, Register Short Indexed, 64bit Register Indirect, 64bit Two-Registers Indexed, 64bit Register Indirect with Post-Increment

Cycles:

Flags affected: Zero is set if Destination=0 and reset otherwise; HalfCarry is set and AddSub is reset (if F bit is set)

TB   **Test Bit**

Opcode   **32**

Format:

0	1	1	0	0	1	0	F	S	S	x	D	D	D	D	d	d	d	d	d	S	S	S	S	s	s	s	s	s	r	r	r
0	1	1	0	0	1	0	F	S	S	x	D	D	D	D	d	d	d	d	d	0	0	0	0	n	n	n	n	n	n	n	n

Performs: Tests Destination Bit, as specified by Source.
Operands size: Byte, Word, Double-Word, Quadruple-Word
Addressing modes:

source: Immediate-8, Immediate, Register, Register Indirect with or without Pre-or-Post-Increment-or-Decrement, Indexed, Register Indexed, Two-Registers Indexed, 64bit Register Indirect, 64bit Two-Registers Indexed, 64bit Register Indirect with Post-Increment

destination: Register, Register Indirect with or without Pre-or-Post-Increment-or-Decrement, Indexed, Register Indexed, Two-Registers Indexed, Register Short Indexed, 64bit Register Indirect, 64bit Two-Registers Indexed, 64bit Register Indirect with Post-Increment

Cycles:

Flags affected: Zero is set if Destination bit=0 and reset otherwise; Carry is set to the value of tested bit; HalfCarry is set and AddSub is reset (if F bit is set)

BINS   Bit Insert
Opcode   **33**

Format:

0	1	1	0	0	1	1	F	S	S	x	D	D	D	D	d	d	d	d	d	S	S	S	S	s	s	s	s	s	r	r	r

Performs: Inserts Bits from Source into Destination, starting at a given point.
Operands size: Double-Word, Quadruple-Word
Addressing modes:

source: Immediate-8, Immediate, Register, Register Indirect with or without Pre-or-Post-Increment-or-Decrement, Indexed, Register Indexed, Two-Registers Indexed, 64bit Register Indirect, 64bit Two-Registers Indexed, 64bit Register Indirect with Post-Increment

destination: Register, Register Indirect with or without Pre-or-Post-Increment-or-Decrement, Indexed, Register Indexed, Two-Registers Indexed, Register Short Indexed, 64bit Register Indirect, 64bit Two-Registers Indexed, 64bit Register Indirect with Post-Increment

Cycles:

Flags affected: Zero is set if Destination=0 and reset otherwise, Sign is affected according to Destination (if F bit is set)

Notes: Control Word comes either from register R1-R7 if r bits are different from 000, otherwise a double-word follows the instruction; Byte 0 of the Control Word specifies Starting Position (0..63), and Byte 1 Number of Bits to be Extracted (0..63); MSB of Byte 3 controls sign-extension, and its b6 specifies if Inserted Bits shall expand to the whole destination space

BXTR   Bit Extract
Opcode   **34**

Format: | 0 | 1 | 1 | 0 | 1 | 0 | 0 | F | S | S | x | D | D | D | D | d | d | d | d | d | S | S | S | S | s | s | s | s | s | r | r | r |

Performs: Extracts Bits from Source into Destination, starting at a given point; sign is extended if MSB of Control Word is set.
Operands size: Double-Word, Quadruple-Word
Addressing modes:
    source: Immediate-8, Immediate, Register, Register Indirect with or without Pre-or-Post-Increment-or-Decrement, Indexed, Register Indexed, Two-Registers Indexed, 64bit Register Indirect, 64bit Two-Registers Indexed, 64bit Register Indirect with Post-Increment
    destination: Register, Register Indirect with or without Pre-or-Post-Increment-or-Decrement, Indexed, Register Indexed, Two-Registers Indexed, Register Short Indexed, 64bit Register Indirect, 64bit Two-Registers Indexed, 64bit Register Indirect with Post-Increment

Cycles:

Flags affected: Zero is set if Destination=0 and reset otherwise, Sign is affected according to Destination (if F bit is set)

Notes: Control Word comes either from register R1-R7 if r bits are different from 000, otherwise a double-word follows the instruction; Byte 0 of the Control Word specifies Starting Position (0..63), and Byte 1 Number of Bits to be Extracted (0..63); MSB of Byte 3 controls sign-extension

BSFR   Bit Search Forward or Reverse
Opcode   35

Format: | 0 | 1 | 1 | 0 | 1 | 0 | 1 | F | S | S | x | D | D | D | D | d | d | d | d | d | S | S | S | S | s | s | s | s | s | x | t | d |

Performs: Searches Source for the first occurrence of a 0 or 1 bit (as selected) and stores its position into Destination; search can go either from MSB to LSB or viceversa.
Operands size: Double-Word, Quadruple-Word
Addressing modes:
    source: Immediate-8, Immediate, Register, Register Indirect with or without Pre-or-Post-Increment-or-Decrement, Indexed, Register Indexed, Two-Registers Indexed, 64bit Register Indirect, 64bit Two-Registers Indexed, 64bit Register Indirect with Post-Increment
    destination: Register, Register Indirect with or without Pre-or-Post-Increment-or-Decrement, Indexed, Register Indexed, Two-Registers Indexed, Register Short Indexed, 64bit Register Indirect, 64bit Two-Registers Indexed, 64bit Register Indirect with Post-Increment

Cycles:

Flags affected: Zero is set if no bit is found (if F bit is set)

SLA/SRA/SRL/RR/RRC/RL/RLC   **Shift/Rotate Left/Right with and without Carry**

Opcode   **38**

Format:

0	1	1	1	0	0	0	F	S	S	C	D	D	D	D	d	d	d	d	c	c	c	c	T	s	s	s	s	M	M	M

Performs: Shifts or Rotates Destination Bits as specified by Source and M bits (conditional execution is available).

> SLA: Shift Left Arithmetic, Destination is shifted to the left as 0s enter from the right; MSB goes into Carry flag
>
> SRA: Shift Right Arithmetic, Destination is shifted to the right as MSBs is copied from the left; LSB goes into Carry flag
>
> SRL: Shift Right Logical, Destination is shifted to the right as 0s enter from the left; LSB goes into Carry flag
>
> RR: Rotate Right, Destination is shifted to the right as previous LSB is copied into new MSB and Carry flag
>
> RRC: Rotate Right with Carry, Destination is shifted to the right as previous LSB is copied into Carry flag and previous Carry flag becomes new MSB
>
> RL: Rotate Left, Destination is shifted to the left as previous MSB is copied into new LSB and Carry flag
>
> RLC: Rotate Left with Carry, Destination is shifted to the left as previous MSB is copied into Carry flag and previous Carry flag becomes new LSB

Operands size: Byte, Word, Double-Word, Quadruple-Word
Addressing modes:

> source: if T=0, shift/rotate amount is provided by R0-R15 as shown by s bits; otherwise s bits provide literal shift amount
>
> destination: Register, Register Indirect with or without Pre-or-Post-Increment-or-Decrement, Indexed, Register Indexed, Two-Registers Indexed, Register Short Indexed, 64bit Register Indirect, 64bit Two-Registers Indexed, 64bit Register Indirect with Post-Increment

Cycles:

Flags affected: Zero, Sign, Carry; HalfCarry is reset (if F bit is set)

MAS   **Multiply, Add and Store**

Opcode   **3C**

Format:

0	1	1	1	1	0	0	F	S	S	M	D	D	D	D	d	d	d	d	d	S	S	S	S	s	s	s	s	s	r	r	r
0	1	1	1	1	0	0	F	S	S	M	D	D	D	D	d	d	d	d	d	S	S	S	S	n	n	n	n	n	n	n	n

Performs: Multiplies Destination and Source, then optionally Adds Operand and finally stores the result back into Destination.
Operands size: Byte, Word, Double-Word, Quadruple-Word
Addressing modes:

> source: Immediate-8, Immediate, Register, Register Indirect with or without Pre-or-Post-Increment-or-Decrement, Indexed, Register Indexed, Two-Registers Indexed, 64bit Register Indirect, 64bit Two-Registers Indexed, 64bit Register Indirect with Post-Increment

destination: Register, Register Indirect with or without Pre-or-Post-Increment-or-Decrement, Indexed, Register Indexed, Two-Registers Indexed, Register Short Indexed, 64bit Register Indirect, 64bit Two-Registers Indexed, 64bit Register Indirect with Post-Increment

Cycles:

Flags affected: Zero, Sign, Carry (if F bit is set)

Notes: if Operand is used, Immediate-8 won't be allowed as a source (and the same goes for all Two-Registers addressing modes)

MSS   Multiply, Subtract and Store
Opcode   **3D**

Format:

0	1	1	1	1	0	0	F	S	S	M	D	D	D	D	d	d	d	d	d	S	S	S	S	s	s	s	s	s	r	r	r
0	1	1	1	1	0	0	F	S	S	M	D	D	D	D	d	d	d	d	d	S	S	S	S	n	n	n	n	n	n	n	n

Performs: Multiplies Destination and Source (optionally negated), then Subtracts Operand and finally stores the result back into Destination.
Operands size: Byte, Word, Double-Word, Quadruple-Word
Addressing modes:
    source: Immediate-8, Immediate, Register, Register Indirect with or without Pre-or-Post-Increment-or-Decrement, Indexed, Register Indexed, Two-Registers Indexed, 64bit Register Indirect, 64bit Two-Registers Indexed, 64bit Register Indirect with Post-Increment
    destination: Register, Register Indirect with or without Pre-or-Post-Increment-or-Decrement, Indexed, Register Indexed, Two-Registers Indexed, Register Short Indexed, 64bit Register Indirect, 64bit Two-Registers Indexed, 64bit Register Indirect with Post-Increment

Cycles:

Flags affected: Zero, Sign, Carry (if F bit is set)

Notes: if Operand is used, Immediate-8 won't be allowed as a source (and the same goes for all Two-Registers addressing modes)

SSA   Square, Sum and Accumulate
Opcode   **3E**

Format:

0	1	1	1	1	1	0	F	S	S	M	D	D	D	D	d	d	d	d	d	S	S	S	S	s	s	s	s	s	r	r	r
0	1	1	1	1	0	0	F	S	S	M	D	D	D	D	d	d	d	d	d	S	S	S	S	n	n	n	n	n	n	n	n

Performs: Calculates Square of Source, optionally Adding Square of Operand and finally Adds Destination and stores the result back into Destination
Operands size: Byte, Word, Double-Word, Quadruple-Word
Addressing modes:

source: Immediate-8, Immediate, Register, Register Indirect with or without Pre-or-Post-Increment-or-Decrement, Indexed, Register Indexed, Two-Registers Indexed, 64bit Register Indirect, 64bit Two-Registers Indexed, 64bit Register Indirect with Post-Increment

destination: Register, Register Indirect with or without Pre-or-Post-Increment-or-Decrement, Indexed, Register Indexed, Two-Registers Indexed, Register Short Indexed, 64bit Register Indirect, 64bit Two-Registers Indexed, 64bit Register Indirect with Post-Increment

Cycles:

Flags affected: Zero, Sign, Carry (if F bit is set)

Notes: if Operand is used, Immediate-8 won't be allowed as a source (and the same goes for all Two-Registers addressing modes)

VMA   Vector Multiply and Add
Opcode   **3F**

Format:

0	1	1	1	1	0	1	M	S	S	x	D	D	D	D	d	d	d	d	d	S	S	S	S	s	s	s	s	s	r	r	r
0	1	1	1	1	1	1	M	S	S	x	D	D	D	D	d	d	d	d	d	S	S	S	S	n	n	n	n	n	n	n	n

Performs: Multiplies all elements of vector pointed at by Destination (whose size is specified by following word) by Source and optionally Adds Operand
Operands size: Byte, Word, Double-Word, Quadruple-Word
Addressing modes:
source: Immediate-8, Immediate, Register, Register Indirect with or without Pre-or-Post-Increment-or-Decrement, Indexed, Register Indexed, Two-Registers Indexed, 64bit Register Indirect, 64bit Two-Registers Indexed, 64bit Register Indirect with Post-Increment
destination: Register Indirect with or without Post-Increment, Indexed, Register Indexed, Register Short Indexed, 64bit Register Indirect, 64bit Register Indirect with Post-Increment

Cycles:

Flags affected: Direction, AddSub and HalfCarry are reset

Notes: if Operand is used, Immediate-8 won't be allowed as a source (and the same goes for all Two-Registers addressing modes)

JMP   Absolute Jump
Opcode   **40**

Format:

1	0	0	0	0	0	0	F	1	x	C	D	D	D	D	d	d	d	d	d	c	c	c	c	x	x	x	x	x	r	r	r

Performs: Jumps to specified address (conditional execution is available).

Operands size: Double-Word, Quadruple-Word
Addressing modes:
> Absolute, Absolute-64, Register, Register Indirect with or without Pre-or-Post-Increment-or-Decrement, Indexed, Register Indexed, Two-Registers Indexed, Register Short Indexed, 64bit Register Indirect, 64bit Two-Registers Indexed, 64bit Register Indirect with Post-Increment

Cycles:

Flags affected: none

Notes: when a register-indexed addressing mode is specified, register value is implicitly multiplied by 4, to ease the creation of jump tables and alike

CALL/BL   Call / Branch and Link
Opcode   **41**

Format:

| 1 | 0 | 0 | 0 | 0 | 0 | 1 | M | S | S | C | D | D | D | D | d | d | d | d | d | c | c | c | c | x | x | x | x | x | r | r | r |

Performs: Calls subroutine at specified address, saving current PC (after this instruction) into either Stack or register R30, depending upon M bit (conditional execution is available).
Operands size: Byte, Double-Word, Quadruple-Word
Addressing modes:
> Absolute, Absolute-64 (only CALL), Register, Register Indirect with or without Pre-or-Post-Increment-or-Decrement, Indexed, Register Indexed, Two-Registers Indexed, Register Short Indexed, 64bit Register Indirect (only CALL), 64bit Two-Registers Indexed, 64bit Register Indirect with Post-Increment (only CALL)

Cycles:

Flags affected: none

Notes: if Size is set to Byte, subroutine address is calculated as current PC plus signed offset; otherwise, absolute value will be used;
> when a register-indexed addressing mode is specified, register value is implicitly multiplied by 4, to ease the creation of jump tables and alike

BLWP   Branch and Link with Workspace
Opcode   **42**

Format:

| 1 | 0 | 0 | 0 | 0 | 0 | 1 | 0 | M | 1 | x | C | D | D | D | D | d | d | d | d | d | c | c | c | c | x | x | x | x | x | r | r | r |

Performs: Calls subroutine at specified address, saving current PC (after this instruction) into either Stack or register R30, depending upon M bit; WP register is loaded with the value at given address and previous WP is stored in R29; Status is saved in R28 (conditional execution is available).
Operands size: Double-Word, Quadruple-Word
Addressing modes:
    Absolute, Register, Register Indirect with or without Pre-or-Post-Increment-or-Decrement, Indexed, Register Indexed, Two-Registers Indexed, Register Short Indexed, Two-Registers Short Indexed

Cycles:

Flags affected: none

Note: this instruction is only valid when Register Remapping is active. RTWP must be used to return control to main program.

RET   Return from Subroutine
Opcode   **43**

Format:

1	0	0	0	0	1	1	T	0	0	C	D	D	D	D	d	d	d	d	d	c	c	c	c	n	n	n	n	n	n	n	n

Performs: Returns control to main program after a subroutine call, and optionally stores provided 8bit number into Destination (conditional execution is available).
Operands size: Byte
Addressing modes:
    Implicit (with optional Immediate value)

Cycles:

Flags affected: none

Note: this instruction is only valid when Register Remapping is active. RTWP must be used to return control to main program.

ENTER   Allocate Stack Area
Opcode   **44**

Format:

1	0	0	0	1	0	0	F	S	S	x	D	D	D	D	d	d	d	d	d	S	S	S	S	s	s	s	s	s	r	r	r

Performs: Allocates space on the Stack, saving given Register onto Stack, SP into that Register and then subtracting given amount of bytes from SP.
Operands size: Byte, Word, Double-Word, Quadruple-Word
Addressing modes:

source: Immediate-8, Immediate, Register, Register Indirect with or without Pre-or-Post-Increment-or-Decrement, Indexed, Register Indexed, Two-Registers Indexed, 64bit Register Indirect, 64bit Two-Registers Indexed, 64bit Register Indirect with Post-Increment
destination: Register

Cycles:

Flags affected: Zero, Sign, Parity (if F bit is set)

LEAVE   Free Stack Area
Opcode   45

Format: | 1 | 0 | 0 | 0 | 1 | 0 | 1 | x | x | x | x | D | D | D | D | d | d | d | d | d | x | x | x | x | x | x | x | x | x | x | x | x |

Performs: Frees space on the Stack, restoring SP from given Register and then previous Register value from the Stack.
Operands size: n/a
Addressing modes:
    Register

Cycles:

Flags affected: none

CHK   Check Array Bounds
Opcode   46

Format: | 1 | 0 | 0 | 0 | 1 | 1 | 0 | F | S | S | x | D | D | D | D | d | d | d | d | d | S | S | S | S | s | s | s | s | s | r | r | r |

Performs: Checks given Destination value against Source, and if it's found higher than that or lower than 0 an Out-Of-Bounds exception is generated.
Operands size: Byte, Word, Double-Word, Quadruple-Word
Addressing modes:
    source: Immediate, Register, Register Indirect with or without Pre-or-Post-Increment-or-Decrement, Indexed, Register Indexed, Two-Registers Indexed, 64bit Register Indirect, 64bit Two-Registers Indexed, 64bit Register Indirect with Post-Increment
    destination: Register, Register Indirect with or without Pre-or-Post-Increment-or-Decrement, Indexed, Register Indexed, Two-Registers Indexed, Register Short Indexed, 64bit Register Indirect, 64bit Two-Registers Indexed, 64bit Register Indirect with Post-Increment

Cycles:

Flags affected: Zero, Sign, Parity (if F bit is set)

X   Execute

Opcode   **47**

Format:

1	0	0	0	1	1	1	x	1	0	x	D	D	D	D	d	d	d	d	d	S	S	S	S	s	s	s	s	s	r	r	r

Performs: Executes Instruction (op-code) given in Source, passing Destination value as a parameter.
Operands size: Double-Word
Addressing modes:

    <u>source</u>: Immediate, Register, Register Indirect with or without Pre-or-Post-Increment-or-Decrement, Indexed, Register Indexed, Two-Registers Indexed, 64bit Register Indirect, 64bit Two-Registers Indexed, 64bit Register Indirect with Post-Increment

    <u>destination</u>: Register, Register Indirect with or without Pre-or-Post-Increment-or-Decrement, Indexed, Register Indexed, Two-Registers Indexed, Register Short Indexed, 64bit Register Indirect, 64bit Two-Registers Indexed, 64bit Register Indirect with Post-Increment

Cycles:

Flags affected: depending upon instruction to be executed.

PUSH   Push value onto Stack

Opcode   **48**

Format:

1	0	0	1	0	0	0	F	S	S	x	x	x	x	x	x	x	x	x	x	S	S	S	S	s	s	s	s	s	r	r	r

Performs: Pushes given value onto the Stack, subracting appropriate number of bytes from it.
Operands size: Byte, Word, Double-Word, Quadruple-Word
Addressing modes:

    <u>source</u>: Immediate-8, Immediate, Register, Register Indirect with or without Pre-or-Post-Increment-or-Decrement, Indexed, Register Indexed, Two-Registers Indexed, 64bit Register Indirect, 64bit Two-Registers Indexed, 64bit Register Indirect with Post-Increment

Cycles:

Flags affected: none.

POP   Pop value from Stack

Opcode   **49**

Format:

1	0	0	1	0	0	1	F	S	S	D	D	D	D	d	d	d	d	d	x	x	x	x	x	x	x	x	x	x	r	r	r

Performs: Pops out a value from the Stack, adding number of bytes to it.
Operands size: Byte, Word, Double-Word, Quadruple-Word
Addressing modes:
    destination: Register, Register Indirect with or without Pre-or-Post-Increment-or-Decrement, Indexed, Register Indexed, Two-Registers Indexed, 64bit Register Indirect, 64bit Two-Registers Indexed, 64bit Register Indirect with Post-Increment

Cycles:

Flags affected: Zero, Sign, Parity (if F bit is set)

LDM   Load Multiple Registers
Opcode   4C

Format:

1	0	0	1	1	0	0	F	1	x	D	D	D	D	d	d	d	d	d	x	x	x	x	x	n	n	n	n	n	n	n	n

Performs: Loads registers from memory at a given address, according to a provided register mask bitfield.
Operands size: Byte, Word, Double-Word, Quadruple-Word
Addressing modes:
    source: Register Indirect with Pre-or-Post-Increment-or-Decrement
    destination/register mask: either 8bit or 32bit

Cycles:

Flags affected: Dir (if F bit is set)

STM   Store Multiple Registers
Opcode   4D

Format:

1	0	0	1	1	0	1	F	1	x	D	D	D	D	d	d	d	d	d	x	x	x	x	x	n	n	n	n	n	n	n	n

Performs: Stores registers to memory at a given address, according to a provided register mask bitfield.
Operands size: Byte, Word, Double-Word, Quadruple-Word
Addressing modes:
    destination: Register Indirect with Pre-or-Post-Increment-or-Decrement
    source/register mask: either 8bit or 32bit

Cycles:

Flags affected: Dir (if F bit is set)

BEQ/BNE/BC/BNC/BMI/BPL/BV/BNV/BHI/BLS/BGE/BLT/BGT/BLE/BPE/BPO
Branch on condition

Opcode   **50**

Format:

1	0	1	0	0	0	0	x	x	x	1	n	n	n	n	n	n	n	n	n	c	c	c	c	n	n	n	n	n	n	n	n

Performs: Branches (jumps) to new address if condition is met; address is relative to current PC+4 and offset is generated using 17bits, treated as a signed number.

$cccc =$ 0000 branch is taken if Z flag is set (jump on zero)
              0001 branch is taken if Z flag is reset (jump on non-zero)
              0010 branch is taken if C flag is set (jump on carry)
              0011 branch is taken if C flag is reset (jump on no-carry)
              0100 branch is taken if S flag is set (jump on negative)
              0101 branch is taken if S flag is reset (jump on positive)
              0110 branch is taken if V flag is set (jump on overflow)
              0111 branch is taken if V flag is reset (jump on no overflow)
              1000 branch is taken if C flag is set and Z is reset (jump on unsigned higher)
              1001 branch is taken if C flag is reset and Z is set (jump on unsigned lower or zero)
              1010 branch is taken if S flag equals V flag (jump on signed greater or equal)
              1011 branch is taken if S flag differs from V flag (jump on signed less than)
              1100 branch is taken if Z flag is set and S flag equals V flag (jump on signed greater than)
              1101 branch is taken if Z flag is set and S flag differs from V flag (jump on signed less than or equal)
              1110 branch is taken if P flag is set (jump on parity even)
              1111 branch is taken if P flag is reset (jump on parity odd)

Operands size: n/a
Addressing modes:
    17bits PC-relative

Cycles:

Flags affected: none

JR   Relative Jump

Opcode   **50**

Format:

1	0	1	0	0	0	0	x	x	x	0	n	n	n	n	n	n	n	n	n	x	x	x	x	n	n	n	n	n	n	n	n

Performs: Branches (jumps) to new address relative to current PC+4, generated using 17bits treated as a signed number.

Operands size: n/a
Addressing modes:
    17bits PC-relative

Cycles:

Flags affected: none

DJNZ   Decrement and Jump if not Zero
Opcode   51

Format:

1	0	1	0	0	0	1	F	S	S	x	D	D	D	D	d	d	d	d	d	S	S	S	S	s	s	s	s	s	r	r	r

Performs: Decrements Destination by 1 and Jumps at provided address if resulting value is non-zero; address is relative to current PC+4 and if Source addressing mode is Immediate an 8bit signed value is used, otherwise a 32bit one.

Operands size: Byte, Word, Double-Word, Quadruple-Word
Addressing modes:
    source/jump address: Immediate-8, Immediate, Register, Register Indirect with or without Pre-or-Post-Increment-or-Decrement, Indexed, Register Indexed, Two-Registers Indexed, 64bit Register Indirect, 64bit Two-Registers Indexed, 64bit Register Indirect with Post-Increment
    destination: Register, Register Indirect with or without Pre-or-Post-Increment-or-Decrement, Indexed, Register Indexed, Two-Registers Indexed, Register Short Indexed, 64bit Register Indirect, 64bit Two-Registers Indexed, 64bit Register Indirect with Post-Increment

Cycles:

Flags affected: Zero, Sign, Parity (if F bit is set)

SKIP   Skip Instructions
Opcode   52

Format:

1	0	1	0	0	1	0	x	0	0	x	x	x	x	x	x	x	x	x	x	x	c	c	c	c	n	n	n	n	n	n	n	n

Performs: Skips given number of instructions if condition is met.

Operands size: Byte
Addressing modes:
    Immediate-8

Cycles:

Flags affected: none

TRAP — Trap

Opcode **6F**

Format:

1	1	0	1	1	1	1	x	0	0	C	x	x	x	x	x	x	x	x	x	c	c	c	c	0	0	n	n	n	n	n	n

Performs: Executes Trap handler at 0x200+n*8 if condition is met (conditional execution available).

Operands size: Byte
Addressing modes:
    Immediate-8

Cycles:

Flags affected: Trap

TRAPV — Trap on Overflow flag

Opcode **6F**

Format:

1	1	0	1	1	1	1	x	0	0	C	x	x	x	x	x	x	x	x	x	c	c	c	c	1	0	x	x	x	x	x	x

Performs: Executes Trap handler at 0x230 if condition is met and/or Overflow flag is set

Operands size: n/a
Addressing modes: n/a

Cycles:

Flags affected: Trap

LDIM — Load Interrupt Mask (privileged instruction)

Opcode **70**

Format:

1	1	1	0	0	0	0	x	0	0	x	x	x	x	x	x	x	x	x	x	S	S	S	S	s	s	s	s	s	r	r	r

Performs: Loads Interrupt Mask with the new value provided.

Operands size: Byte
Addressing modes:
   source: Immediate-8, Register, Register Indirect with or without Pre-or-Post-Increment-or-Decrement, Indexed, Register Indexed, Two-Registers Indexed, 64bit Register Indirect, 64bit Two-Registers Indexed, 64bit Register Indirect with Post-Increment

Cycles:

Flags affected: none

LDST   Load Status Register (privileged instruction*)
Opcode   **71**

Format: | 1 | 1 | 1 | 0 | 0 | 0 | 0 | 0 | S | S | x | x | x | x | x | x | x | x | x | x | S | S | S | S | s | s | s | s | s | r | r | r |

Performs: Sets Status bits to the new value provided, affecting either only lower 8bits (valid also in non-supervisor mode) or the whole 32.

Operands size: Byte, Double-Word
Addressing modes:
   source: Immediate-8, Immediate, Register, Register Indirect with or without Pre-or-Post-Increment-or-Decrement, Indexed, Register Indexed, Two-Registers Indexed, 64bit Register Indirect, 64bit Two-Registers Indexed, 64bit Register Indirect with Post-Increment

Cycles:

Flags affected: all

LDSP   Load Stack Pointer (privileged instruction)
Opcode   **72**

Format: | 1 | 1 | 1 | 0 | 0 | 0 | 1 | 0 | S | S | x | x | x | x | x | x | x | x | x | 1 | q | S | S | S | S | s | s | s | s | s | r | r | r |

Performs: Loads SP (Stack Pointer) with the new value provided: Supervisor SP is affected if q=1, otherwise User SP.

Operands size: Double-Word
Addressing modes:
   source: Immediate-8, Immediate, Register, Register Indirect with or without Pre-or-Post-Increment-or-Decrement, Indexed, Register Indexed, Two-Registers Indexed, 64bit Register Indirect, 64bit Two-Registers Indexed, 64bit Register Indirect with Post-Increment

Cycles:

Flags affected: none

LDWP   Load Workspace (privileged instruction)
Opcode   **72**

Format:

1	1	1	0	0	0	1	0	S	S	x	x	x	x	x	x	x	x	0	0	S	S	S	S	s	s	s	s	s	r	r	r

Performs: Loads WP (Workspace Pointer) with the new value provided.

Operands size: Double-Word
Addressing modes:
     source: Immediate-8, Immediate, Register, Register Indirect with or without Pre-or-Post-Increment-or-Decrement, Indexed, Register Indexed, Two-Registers Indexed, 64bit Register Indirect, 64bit Two-Registers Indexed, 64bit Register Indirect with Post-Increment

Cycles:

Flags affected: none

STST   Store Status Register
Opcode   **73**

Format:

1	1	1	0	0	1	0	0	S	S	x	D	D	D	D	d	d	d	d	d	x	x	x	x	x	x	x	x	x	r	r	r

Performs: Stores Status register to the provided Destination (either lower 8 bits, User-mode flags, or all 32).

Operands size: Byte, Double-Word
Addressing modes:
     destination: Register, Register Indirect with or without Pre-or-Post-Increment-or-Decrement, Indexed, Register Indexed, Two-Registers Indexed, 64bit Register Indirect, 64bit Two-Registers Indexed, 64bit Register Indirect with Post-Increment

Cycles:

Flags affected: none

STSP — Store Stack Pointer

Opcode **74**

Format:

1	1	1	0	1	0	0	0	1	0	x	D	D	D	D	d	d	d	d	d	x	x	x	x	x	x	0	0	0	r	r	r

Performs: Stores current Stack Pointer (either Supervisor or User) register to the provided Destination.

Operands size: Double-Word
Addressing modes:
   destination: Register, Register Indirect with or without Pre-or-Post-Increment-or-Decrement, Indexed, Register Indexed, Two-Registers Indexed, 64bit Register Indirect, 64bit Two-Registers Indexed, 64bit Register Indirect with Post-Increment

Cycles:

Flags affected: none

STWP — Store Workspace

Opcode **74**

Format:

1	1	1	0	1	0	0	0	1	0	x	D	D	D	D	d	d	d	d	d	x	x	x	x	x	x	0	0	1	r	r	r

Performs: Stores Workspace Pointer register to the provided Destination.

Operands size: Double-Word
Addressing modes:
   destination: Register, Register Indirect with or without Pre-or-Post-Increment-or-Decrement, Indexed, Register Indexed, Two-Registers Indexed, 64bit Register Indirect, 64bit Two-Registers Indexed, 64bit Register Indirect with Post-Increment

Cycles:

Flags affected: none

STEX — Store Exception state

Opcode **74**

Format:

1	1	1	0	1	0	0	0	1	0	x	D	D	D	D	d	d	d	d	d	x	x	x	x	x	x	1	n	n	r	r	r

Performs: Stores selected Exception state register to the provided Destination.

Operands size: Double-Word
Addressing modes:
    destination: Register, Register Indirect with or without Pre-or-Post-Increment-or-Decrement, Indexed, Register Indexed, Two-Registers Indexed, 64bit Register Indirect, 64bit Two-Registers Indexed, 64bit Register Indirect with Post-Increment

Cycles:

Flags affected: none

RTWP   Return with Workspace (privileged instruction)
Opcode   **75**

Format:

1	1	1	0	1	0	1	M	x	x	C	x	x	x	x	x	x	x	x	x	x	c	c	c	c	c	x	x	x	x	x	x	x	x

Performs: Reverts BLWP instruction, restoring Status register from R28, Program Counter from either SP or R30 (according to M bit) and in the end WP (Workspace Pointer) from R29 (conditional execution is available).
Operands size: n/a
Addressing modes:
    n/a

Cycles:

Flags affected: none

RETI   Return from Interrupt or Exception (privileged instruction)
Opcode   **76**

Format:

1	1	1	0	1	1	0	0	x	x	x	x	x	x	x	x	x	x	x	x	x	x	x	x	x	x	x	x	x	x	x	x	x	x

Performs: Returns from an Interrupt or Exception handler.

Operands size: n/a
Addressing modes:
    n/a

Cycles:

Flags affected: all (restored)

(reserved for cache and atomic operations management)

XOP — Execute Operation

Opcode   **7E**

Format: | 1 | 1 | 1 | 1 | 1 | 1 | 1 | 0 | x | 1 | 0 | x | D | D | D | D | d | d | d | d | d | S | S | S | S | s | s | s | s | r | r | r |

Performs: Executes Privileged Operation (like a Trap) but also handles WP register in a similar way to BLWP instruction; then jumps at the handler at 0x100+n*8.

Operands size: DWORD
Addressing modes:
  source/XOP code: Immediate-8, Immediate, Register, Register Indirect with or without Pre-or-Post-Increment-or-Decrement, Indexed, Register Indexed, Two-Registers Indexed, 64bit Register Indirect, 64bit Two-Registers Indexed, 64bit Register Indirect with Post-Increment
  destination: Register
  32bit parameter follows

Cycles:

Flags affected: XOP

HALT — Halt CPU

Opcode   **7F**

Format: | 1 | 1 | 1 | 1 | 1 | 1 | 1 | 1 | x | x | x | C | x | x | x | x | x | x | x | x | x | c | c | c | c | x | x | x | x | x | x | x |

Performs: Halts CPU, if condition is met.

Operands size: n/a
Addressing modes:
  n/a

Cycles:

Flags affected: none

:

Table of Contents

www.ingramcontent.com/pod-product-compliance
Lightning Source LLC
LaVergne TN
LVHW051623050326
832903LV00033B/4637